mini

Osprey Colour Series

mini

MARK STEWARD

Published in 1989 by Osprey Publishing Limited
Michelin House, 81 Fulham Road,
London SW3 6RB

First reprint spring 1990
Second reprint autumn 1992

British Library Cataloguing in Publication Data

Steward, Mark
    Mini
    I. Title
    629.2′222
    ISBN 0 85045 875 7

Editor Nicholas Collins
Design Martin Richards

Printed in Hong Kong

Title pages
*As well as the works team, private
entries were keen to use the Mini in
rallys.*

Contents

Foreword

I am honoured to have been asked to write the fore-word for this book, *Mini* by Mark Steward.

I think Sir Alec Issigonis who designed the Mini was one of the finest road car designers of all time. He was the first person to design a car the size of a bubble-car but with interior dimensions rivalling those of ordinary saloons. He also pioneered the east-west engine layout, controversial at the time, but since copied by virtually all major manufacturers the world over. A tribute to Sir Alec's genius is the fact the car designed over 30 years ago is still in pro-duction today.

The Mini has been extremely successful in motor sport too. Following the success of the BMC A-series engine in securing the Formula 3 World Champion-ship the birth of the Mini Cooper was a logical step forward. Mini Coopers and Cooper S's enjoyed over-whelming success in both racing and rallying, the victories at Monte Carlo perhaps being the most widely acclaimed.

I look back upon my ten years as consultant to the British Motor Corporation and the racing of Mini Coopers as perhaps one of the best decades of my life.

I am honoured the Mini Cooper has become a col-lector's car the world over and I sincerely hope the continuing popularity of the Mini will ensure produc-tion continues for many years.

John N Cooper.

Introduction

Sir Alec Issigonis – genius behind the Mini.

'What I see before me is only stagnation, everything has been done. Cars will remain as they are, I mean you can't tell one car today from another unless you look at the badge. The only exception is the MINI!'

So said the late Sir Alec Issigonis, the creator of the Mini, on his 80th birthday in 1986. This sentiment is shared by countless numbers of people all over the world who have been enchanted by the magic that is the Mini.

Acknowledgements

Many thanks to everyone who helped in the production of this book, especially the staff of the British Motor Industry Heritage Trust, John Cooper, Jeffrey Archer, and Kevin Jones and Tony Cumming at Austin Rover. Thanks also to members of the London and Surrey Mini Owners Club, Cooper Register, Mini Owners Club and Mini 7 Racing Club for their patience whilst their cars were being photographed. Also Julian Carter, Vicky Steward, Martin Pink, Andrew and Jacky Stanton for editing and general help and support.

Last but not least Paul Debois who took most of the photographs in the book and had to endure spending so much time with Mini freaks (myself included).

To the memory of
Sir Alexander Arnold Constantine Issigonis
1906–1988
Who made it all possible.

Body and soul

Why has the Mini, even with its faults, managed to last three decades? Many would say it is because of Issigonis's design brilliance but that's just too simple. Many top designers have built many classic cars but this has not guaranteed long production runs. A cynical view would be to say that the Mini's long production run is a reflection of bad management in the companies that have produced the Mini over the years, but that would not be totally fair.

A key reason to why the Mini has lasted so long is that many of its features have endeared themselves to the Mini driver. Even owners who go onto bigger cars look for cars with similar driving characteristics, solid suspension, nippy front wheel drive or whatever other virtues they saw in the old 'Min'. Those basic characteristics started as notes on Issigonis's drawing board and ended up as a legend.

The design brief behind the Mini was to design a car to seat four people in comfort but be as small as possible on the outside. It was stated in *Motor* magazine in 1959 that 'we have deliberately made the car very small because we have found new ways of making the inside very big'. Issigonis considered himself an 'Ironmonger' but a more accurate description might be a master craftsman; a master craftsman who brought the parts together and produced the whole – ageless in its simplicity and genius.

The engine used in the Mini since its launch, known as the A-series engine, was one of a family of engines developed by the British Motor Corporation (BMC). It was originally a Austin engine which was first used in the Austin A30 in 1952. However, it looked very different to the Mini configuration because it was mounted in-line, rather than transversely across the car, and had a separate gearbox.

The A-series in different forms was fitted in a number of BMC cars, notably Issigonis's Morris Minor between 1952 and 1956. It is a tribute to Bill Appleby, designer of the A-series engine, that it has lasted nearly four decades. Of course the engine has developed greatly, in 1952 the 803cc block in the A30 produced 25 horsepower, by 1982 the MG Metro Turbo unit was producing 93 horsepower.

For cost reasons, Issigonis was under instructions to use an existing BMC engine when designing the car. BMC had to invest £10 million to equip the plants just to produce the Mini. The engine set-up was not an automatic choice, a two-cylinder air cooled unit was tested first but two cylinders were found to be too rough and air cooling was noisy and inefficient. Once four cylinders and watercooling were decided upon the A-series was the natural candidate, not least because of its size. It was Issigonis who made the radical and untried step of putting the gearbox under the engine block and using the same oil system. It was not totally revolutionary to mount the engine transversely but the marriage between engine and gearbox was, and no doubt Issigonis would have been told that it could not be done. The engine was initially the opposite way round in the engine bay but was turned to give the carburettor and inlet valves some haven from the damp British climate. Racing car constructor and man behind the Mini Cooper, John Cooper, recalls that Issigonis was not particularly keen to use the A-series but was sure he could change it for a new engine of his own design once the car was in production.

Front wheel drive was chosen because it was believed that it would give more room, better road holding, quieter running and better facilities for in-

Cooper S in Monte Carlo trim.

terior heating. The problem faced was that several low priced front-wheel-drive cars at the time suffered from transmission 'snatch' (the steering wheel jerking as the turning front wheels resisted steering on full lock.) It was realised that a new way of passing the engine's power through to the wheels was needed. The answer was found by a company called Hardy Spicer who bought the rights to a design of joint which was intended for submarine conning-towers. In later years Hardy Spicer would supply a similar joint to the world's front-wheel-drive cars.

The Mini's subframes which support the cars mechanics front and rear have also played a big part in the cars success. Issigonis had used independent

subframes rather than the traditional chassis running the length of the car on the Morris Minor but the Mini did not have subframes until quite late in its development. The first running prototypes, nick-named 'orange boxes' because of their distinctive colour, did not have subframes. It was found that the chassis structure which was part welded to the orange boxes caused metal fatigue at the locating points. So subframes were used to overcome this and had the added advantage of producing a quieter ride. The importance of subframes to the Mini's success lays in its adaptability. A subframe of 1959 looks remarkably the same as a subframe of today but over the years, the frames have supported many different features and made others possible. The adaptability of the Mini subframe is demonstrated by their use in many homemade kit cars.

Although the A-series engine was not designed for the Mini it has proved itself an ideal power plant.

The first wheels fitted to the Mini were of 10 inch diameter. This was to minimize the amount of room taken up by wheel arches and so leave more room inside. Although small wheels and tyres had been fitted to what are today called micro-cars (such as the Reliant three wheeler) the Mini's 10 inch wheels and tyres were three inches smaller than that of the Austin A35 and a whole 5 inches smaller than the Renault Dauphine (one of the Mini's main rivals). Producing a small tyre which would last for a reason-

able mileage was not easy and close cooperation was called for between the Mini team and Dunlop. It is said that when Dunlop were asked for the tyres Issigonis held out his hands and said that he wanted the tyres 'this big', there being 10 inches between his outstretched hands. The car's small wheels were quite a talking point and some sceptics just did not believe the small tyres would last more than a few thousand miles. Issigonis carried around in his jacket pocket a photograph to answer the sceptics, a picture of a Mini fitted with wheels and tyres off an old Austin 7, nearly twice the size of the Mini's. If anyone said anything to Issigonis about the Mini's wheel size he would show the photograph and say how silly the car would look if it had big wheels. It was not until 1974 that the 1275GT model became the first production Mini to have 12 inch wheels and tyres, when there was the optional extra of Dunlop Denovos which allowed you to deive on after a blow out. The Denovo did not last long as it expired with the 1275GT in 1980. This was mainly due to the extra cost involved. For the same reason 1275GT owners today more often than not do not replace Denovos but switch to ordinary 12 inch wheels. Indeed, since 1984 all Minis have run on 12 inch wheels. Some enthusiasts are now converting their cars to 13 inch wheels shod with ultra-low profile tyres, despite the fact that one such tyre can cost as much as a set of 10 inch tyres.

The braking on Minis started with 7 inch drum brakes all round. The first improvement to them was in 1964 when the front brake changed to having two wheel cylinders rather than the one fitted before. Alongside this the production of higher performance Minis called for better braking. When, in 1961, the first Mini Cooper was introduced, it was clear that improved handling and speed characteristics needed improved braking to match. The then newly developed Lockheed disc brakes were chosen to replace the front drums. The braking was greatly enhanced as the wearing surface on the brakes was twice that of the drums. Lockheed were more than happy to help John Cooper as he convinced them that if the system could work on the Mini using tiny 7 inch

discs it would be a great advertisement for them. The Cooper S introduced in 1963 called for even better brake performance; this was achieved by increasing the discs to 7.5 inches and increasing their thickness. A servo-booster was also added to reduce the pressure needed on the pedal. The 12 inch wheels introduced on the GT pioneered the way for the larger 8.4 inch disc brakes still used on Minis today.

The suspension system for the first Mini, like many other features of the car, was revolutionary. The independent rubber suspension was developed by Moulton Developments Ltd at Bradford-on-Avon. The company, which was founded by Sir Leonard Lord (the chairman of BMC) to develop components for BMC cars, was headed by Alex Moulton who had worked with Issigonis on earlier projects. Although the Mini's ride is often criticised today, in 1959 its ride was considered very impressive. *Motor* enthused in its issue of August 26th 1959 'Experience of the back seat ride in very varied conditions emphasised that passengers enjoy smoother riding in this car than in the back seats of most models costing twice as much.' The Mini suspension system has not changed greatly, apart from the years 1964 to 1971 when 'hydrolastic' suspension was used. Simply put, a water and anti-freeze mixture was contained under pressure within sealed units on each side of the car. When the front of the car hit a bump in the road some of the liquid was displaced to the back, lifting the suspension and levelling the car. The merits of the system are a matter of argument but it was economics which stopped its used as it was far more expensive than dry suspension.

A key reason the Mini has enjoyed such a long production run and has stayed so popular is that the Mini has never looked out of style with its surroundings even though it has changed very little externally. This is especially strange when you consider that Issigonis was not a stylist saying 'stylists are employed to make things obsolescent – like womens clothes . . . . . I design cars which cannot be obsolescent and therefore give value for money'. Issigonis was above everything an engineer and he designed cars as an engineer.

Hornet

Mk. II

ydrolastic' suspen-
ornet smooth, level,
ng—whatever the

Below
The famous Minilite wheel developed by John Cooper, with the 10 inch tyre which allowed more room in the Mini's interior.

Right
The hydrolastic suspension system as shown in a BMC sales brochure in 1966.

In 1961 the Wolseley Hornet and Riley Elf were introduced to bring a little more style to the Mini. The new styling was not done by Issigonis but the work of designer Dick Burzi. Issigonis was not happy as the increased weight cut performance. Issigonis was only interested in practicality, considering the Mini a 'Tin Box' for moving people from A to B and hopefully back.

The Mini's body is a fairly simple construction of spot welded panels with external seams. It has been said that the idea behind this was so that the car could be produced overseas by workers with less skill than their British counterparts. This does not really ring true; surely it would be better to train the over-seas workers than just make their work easier. Perhaps the answer to the external seams question lies in the fact that Issigonis was fairly limited in his expenditure on the development of the car. As well as designing the car, Issigonis had to produce all the tools, formers and frames to make the car, all of which ate into the budget. When producing the body rather than spend money on expensive jigs to hold the car parts together in the right place, he just folded the seams outward and held parts together with simple clamps. Was it, therefore, just that it was never changed from those early pre-production days?

Below left
The 848cc engine powered the new car to a standing quarter mile time of 23.6sec.

Right
Mini's boot although not large still gave more room for luggage than the bubble cars

Below
The de-luxe models of the Austin 7 and Morris Mini Minor came with carpet and better seats, as well as exterior improvements.

Left
The Mini van was very popular with enterprises of all sizes.

Above
The pickup – the ideal vehicle for small builders.

Mini Countryman had wooden sides which were not structural and were added to give the car traditional looks.

Early days

The launch of the Mini on the 26 August 1959 was an international event with BMC having Minis ready in the showrooms in no less than 100 countries. BMC had been set up in 1952 with the merger of Austin and Morris cars but the dealerships were still separate. This resulted in the Mini being launched under the titles of 'Austin 7' and 'Morris Mini Minor', although differences between them were small and cosmetic. The national papers carried large advertisements announcing the launch of the new British small car which strongly emphasised the car's economy and value for money.

Journalists of the motoring press were very responsive to the new car both from a practical view and a patriotic one. *Motor Sport*, wrote in September 1959 'BMC introduced economy cars which are as original, as up-to-date and as practical as the best models from the leading European factories. MOTOR SPORT has fought for years for a new approach to small-car design by British engineers, in order to combat popularity of Continental best-sellers.' In the same issue they made two predictions; one came true the other unfortunately did not – 'With tuning kits available from specialist sources and their revolutionary cornering power these new cars should make a great impression amongst sports-car drivers and rally competitors.' and 'This vitally new BMC model is not only a completely fresh conception of small car design, but is offered at a sensationally modest price. Under these circumstances, it is difficult to see how sales of Continental small cars can be maintained in this country and America.'

The Autocar was similarly impressed if not in such a flag-waving way. Its 28 August 1959 issue praised the model by writing 'Throwing convention to the wind often produced freaks in the automobile world, but when done by a clever and imaginative designer the result may be outstanding. This is certainly the case with the Morris Mini-Minor which, during a road test of the deluxe model, was found to set new standards of comfort and road worthiness in the very small family car class'.

However, 'the car for the people' was not an overnight success and sales were slow at first. This was mainly due to the car buying public's natural apprehension of anything new. As *Motor* magazine recalled in 1964 'Remember the impact this little car had in 1959. The surprise of everyone at a responsible lot like BMC putting their famous Austin and Morris labels on a comic creation whose engine faced the wrong way; had tiny wheels, no drive shaft down the middle and rubber springs.'

Issigonis designed the Mini to be the car to get the British working classes on the roads but the working class looking for their first car were unsure about parting with their hard earned money on such a small car. To everyone's surprise it was increasingly the trendy middle classes who bought the Mini due to the ease of parking, a great benefit in the London of the early 1960's when parking was perhaps worse than it is now. When Lord Snowdon, who was a close friend of Issigonis, and other notables were spotted driving the Mini, it was said by the man in the street that if 'they' drive them, so can we.

In the two years following the launch BMC added the Minivan, estate and pickup. A big year for the Mini was 1961. The Wolseley Hornet and Riley Elf were launched to give a luxury end to the Mini range. Both cars harked back to days gone by with tailed boot and upright grille and on the inside leather and wood. The Elf and Hornet are often described flippantly as 'badge engineered' following the tradition of BMC cars having Riley and Wolseley versions. This is not totally fair as the cars were very important in the development of the Mini, for example they had the 998cc engine five years before the standard Mini and wind up windows three years before other models. Not to mention the fact that you got an extra 2.5 cubic foot of luggage space. The motoring press were again suitably impressed, *The Autocar* printed this appreciation on 13 October 1961 'It is apparent from the specification that the Wolseley Hornet and Riley Elf will satisfy those small-car buyers who put a premium on finish and comprehensive equipment at the expense of some performance due to extra weight.'

The same year also saw the launch of the 'racey' Mini Cooper. John Cooper was a well known figure in motoring. He was also a World Champion racing car constructor in 1959 and 1960. It was his idea to produce a sporty Mini but why did BMC take up Cooper's ideas? The answer perhaps lies in an *Autocar* article published a week after the Hornet and Elf launch article in 1961. 'From the group of motorists, to whom expense within reason is not the main consideration, has come the main instigation for the performance improvements kits and conversions for Minis and other models which have appeared on the market in the last two years. It is natural, therefore, that the manufacturers themselves, seeing this potential market, should develop a model which would not only give improved performance but would combine with it accepted standards of reliability and, in view of the car's special character, a higher-than-normal level of finish as well.'

Everyone agrees that the appeal of the Cooper was, and still is, its performance – an excellent match between horsepower and road holding. In addition the Cooper has a 'status' to it due to scarcity over and above its performance. An ordinary Mini, given the same performance characteristics, is still

Sales leaflet of the Mk II Hornet.

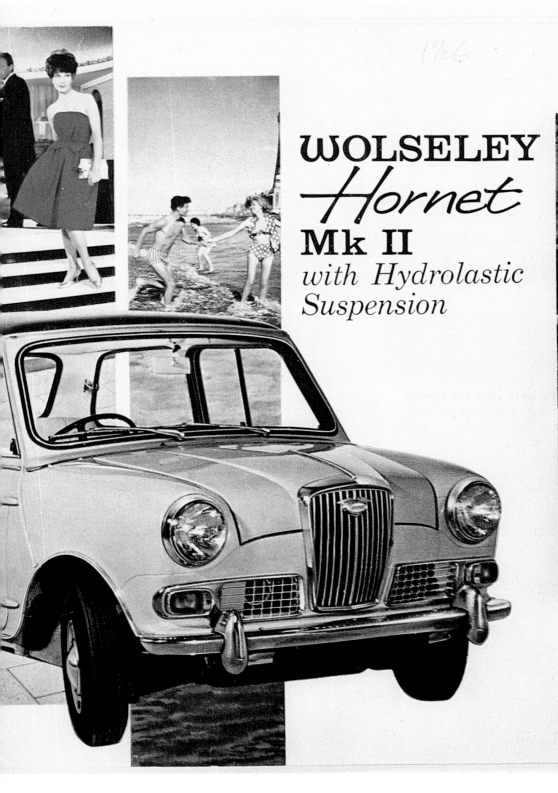

WOLSELEY *Hornet*
Mk II
with Hydrolastic Suspension

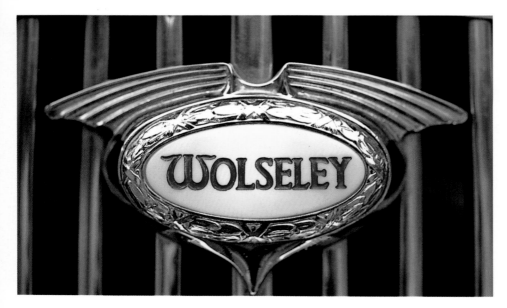

Left
Like earlier Wolseleys the badge on the front grille was illuminated.

Below
The Wolseley and Riley grilles were styled on earlier models.

Below right
Extra room for the luggage or shopping.

879 YKL

'just' a Mini. This is very much seen by the huge prices of original Coopers today.

A very different Mini derivative, the Moke, was launched in 1964. It was developed with a very specific market in mind, that being the armed forces. The idea was to build a sturdy, lightweight go-anywhere vehicle, that could be stacked to save space and parachute dropped to where it was needed. However, it could not go everywhere because its ground clearance was just too low and it did not have the carrying capacity the army was looking for. BMC took a calculated risk in launching the Moke as a fun car ideally suited for hot summer days. The Moke had a canopy to guard against the elements but even with this, it was only the very brave who used it in all weathers. In the 1960's the car became a favourite for the caftan wearing hippie who changed military green paintwork to a psychedelic rainbow of colours. When BMC was replaced by British Leyland the Moke was dropped as it was considered wrong to supply such a small market. However, production continued in Australia and later in Portugal, the Moke developed into a well equipped fun vehicle far better than the original basic military vehicle. All Minis are fun to drive but the Moke, because of its openess, gives a great feel of freedom to the driver.

There comes a time in the development of a car when it is too old to be radical and too young to be classic. For the Mini, this time was, perhaps, the end

of the sixties when Minis were beginning to be criticised in the Motoring press. *Motor* magazine 18 October 1969 being a good example 'Regular readers will have noticed our recent waning enthusiasm for Mini motoring. Make no mistake, we'd be the first to acknowledge the brilliance of the Mini concept and that many detail changes have improved it over the years. The trouble, in our view, is that they haven't improved it enough, particularly in comfort and refinement. Our own comparative group tests have cogently (forcibly) underlined how far the Mini had lagged behind several rivals in these two departments.' Quite damning criticism but they go on to say, 'many of our criticisms have been answered in one go with the introduction of the new long-nose variants which are a lot more civilised and habitable than any previous Mini.' The long-nosed Mini they were referring to was Clubman.

The new nose extended the length of the Mini by just over 4 inches and as well as modernising the car it was said to make it easier to work on the engine and to increase the ability to absorb impact in accidents. The Clubman was introduced alongside the existing Minis (apart from the Hornet and Elf which were dropped) and did not differ greatly in price with other models bearing in mind improved trim, the Clubman being £50 dearer than the Mini Super, the Clubman estate being £70 more than the Mini Traveller and the 1275GT was £108 less than the Cooper S. Although the GT was advertised as a modern sport car it produced 17 bhp less than the S. The Clubman lasted throughout the 70's and ended in 1980 when the more traditional front end continued. Perhaps the Mini had grown old enough to have classical looks.

A Mk III Riley Elf – the Elf was very similar to the Hornet but the Elf enjoyed better interiors.

Below
Austin Cooper Mk I – first of the fast Minis.

Right
The Mk I Cooper had a stylish interior to match its new stylish performance.

Above
Cooper Mk I engine bay showing the twin SU carbs.

Left
The Morris version of the Mk I Cooper.

Above
Distinctive bonnet badge of a Mk II Cooper S.

Right
Morris Cooper S Mk II.

Above
Engine bay of the S – note the servo on right hand side to help brake the increased power output.

Left
The S interior was not as elaborate as earlier Coopers but reclining seats added driver comfort.

Below
Mini Moke.

Following pages
The Moke on the road, the ideal car for feeling the wind in your hair.

Following pages inset
A late Moke – a long way from its original military rôle.

Sell, Sell, Sell,

The Clubman family.

MINI 1275 GT Carries on where the Cooper left off

And how!

All the fun, all the performance wrapped up in a more stylish and comfortable package.

You have 60 spirited horsepower to whip you swiftly past meanderers. You have extra sticky radials on the four corners to hold you firm on corners. You have power-boosted disc/drum braking too to gobble up your speed without drama or fade. And you begin to understand why other manufacturers had to resort to freak 'specials' to stop the Minis winning all the rallies!

Here's proof you don't need cost and complication to enjoy your motoring. You don't need vast bonnets, power bulges, aerofoils, V12s and something from your bank manager.

All you need is the Mini 1275 G.T.

The Mini, despite up and downs, has sold well for nearly three decades and well over 5 million cars have been produced. What part has the marketing and selling machine of the producers played in this?

It is often said that the Mini was created to stem the flood of foreign imports of small cars but this is not completely true. The foreign producers were not set up to import large number of cars into Britain. Indeed it was not until the early 1970's that foreign car imports took off. The few 'bubble cars' which did get to Britain looked very outlandish but there was a market for these cars as they were low priced and importantly, the demand for cars outstripped supply. As the Mini was not much more expensive than the

The 1275GT, better than the Cooper?

bubble cars, the public could buy a true car able to carry four people and luggage as well. The Mini then effectively wiped out the bubble cars as was intended.

The fact that the car is British was no doubt a help both in the home market and overseas. Many people like to purchase British but then again they will not buy just because of this, so the car must stand up to scrutiny. The Mini has never been sold in a patriotic way because the public can take the cynical view that it is being pushed as British

The amount of different badges goes some way to show just how many different models have been made.

because it is not good enough in itself. Research has found that overseas buyers have images of British cars based on Rolls-Royce, Aston Martin, Rovers etc. If you mention British cars to them they think of luxury, comfort and performance. Although they do not expect that from the Mini, there is a kind of 'chic' linked association.

In the early days of the Mini the marketing men did not have as much say as they do today but as already said it was a seller's market. In the 1970's with increasing competition this side of the company gained importance. Today what the buyer wants from a car is all important and marketing and sales have to incorporate these requirements into product planning and on to the production line. For many years the driving force behind the launch of many Mini models were the separate dealerships for Austin, Morris, Riley and Wolseley. In total there were over 6000 dealerships (six times as many as now). This meant that the dealers were in competition with each other.

The 1960's were also the Cooper years. Racing success contributed to the Mini character as David and Goliath battles were waged on the track. There were

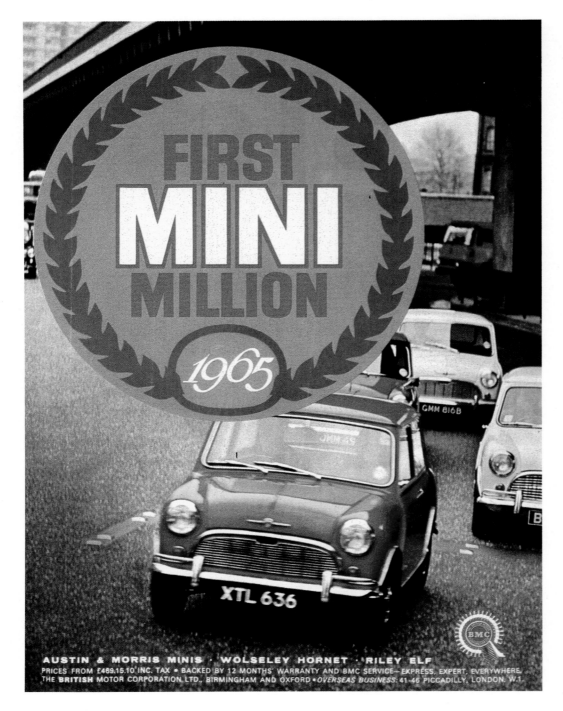

FIRST
MINI
MILLION
1965

AUSTIN & MORRIS MINIS · WOLSELEY HORNET · RILEY ELF
PRICES FROM £469.15.10 INC. TAX · BACKED BY 12 MONTHS' WARRANTY AND BMC SERVICE—EXPRESS, EXPERT, EVERYWHERE.
THE BRITISH MOTOR CORPORATION LTD., BIRMINGHAM AND OXFORD · OVERSEAS BUSINESS: 41-46 PICCADILLY, LONDON, W.1.

Left
Mini's first million – this simple advertisement is typical of early ads.

Right
Even early sales leaflets were simple.

quite high levels of awareness of its racing success amongst the public and sales benefited as a result. When 'The Italian Job' film was made in 1969 the sales of red, white and blue Minis soared, as the film showed just how fast and agile the Mini was.

In 1969 the introduction of the Clubman was an attempt to give the Mini more status. The reason for the front end change was to try and make the car look bigger and therefore more expensive, making the buyer think he was getting more for his money. Of course this is a totally false impression as the interior room was not changed. However, the ordinary Mini shape continued and outlasted the Clubman.

The Clubman fronted 1275GT was to replace the Cooper in the early 1970's. This was soon after the BMC/Leyland merger when accountants were looking critically at costs and as margins were slim it was

AUSTIN **Mini Cooper** Mk II
Mini Cooper 'S' Mk II

42

felt royalties paid to John Cooper could not be justified. At the time when the Cooper S was dropped, the company was only building 23 S's per week. Further, the new boss, Lord Stokes, was just not interested in performance cars as seen by him closing the successful competitions department.

Advertising for the Mini in the 1970's tended to be character-based rather than specification-based as in the 1960's. The reason for this was really two-fold. In the 1970's, it became harder to rationally say that the Mini was the best car to buy when there was some very good competition and also advertising in general had moved to selling a product's character rather than just the product itself. People buy cars for a mix of rational and emotional reasons and by the 1970's the emotional value of the Mini was well known. Even the new generation hatchbacks could not beat this, thus the advertising was built on the character of the car. It did not manufacture an image but reinforced people's established perceptions of the Mini. Also by this time there were more female Mini buyers than males and so the advertisements were tailored accordingy. What the advertising did and continues to do, is remind potential buyers of the model's personality in a way which is interesting, fun and different from other car advertising. For example the 'Minis have feelings too' advertisements could not work with any other car.

When the Metro was launched it was called the MiniMetro and this lead some to believe that was in anticipation of the Metro taking over from the Mini. This was not the case. Austin Rover wanted to call the car Metro from launch but another manufacturer had registered the name. So to get over the problem MiniMetro was chosen. It is true that in the years preceding the launch of the Metro it was planned that it would replace the Mini but market research changed all this. Research showed that there was a section of people who would continue to buy the Mini after the Metro was on sale. These people were broken down into two main groups: the young first time buyer and the second car buyer.

Some Mini adverts have caused a stir.

Their needs and requirements in a car were quite different from those of the small multi-purpose hatchback buyer. The 'hot hatches' and their less potent brethren were being purchased by young couples who had or were about to have a family. The Mini buyer did not want a hatchback; he or she did not want its features or the associated character of the hatchback. This research saved the Mini. Without it, the car would have gone out of production in about 1981.

The latest way of keeping attention is by way of limited edition Minis.The added advantage of this, to Austin Rover at least, is that buyers wanting these cars may purchase a City or Mayfair model if they cannot get the limited edition.

It has often been said that the Mini never made a profit or that it even made a loss. Reasons are then put forward as to why it continued to be made – economies of scale, and introduction to the range or to satisfy the dealerships demand for cars. These misconceptions arose from the findings of accountants who went through the figures at the time of the BMC/Leyland merger. However, if the Mini had not have been making profits, it would have been dropped just as quickly as other models discontinued at the time. The Mini makes profits for Austin Rover now and they strongly suspect it has made profits in the past. After all, would a company continue to sell so many at a loss?

Whilst advertising did not create the Mini character it has played a big part in maintaining it. Recent advertising has been entertaining and very fast to react. In April 1987, the newspapers carried a story about a Great Dane which jumped 30 ft onto a Mini roof. Within days advertisements appeared showing a dazed Mini with the question 'Has anyone spared a thought for the Mini?'

The Mini, perhaps because it came as such a basic car, triggered off a secondary market in accessories the like of which had not been seen before or since. Since the Mini was first launched, owners have been keen to spruce up their cars because it is cheap and easy to do. You name it – you could buy it and put it on your Mini to make you car just a little bit different from every other Mini down your street.

One of a series of ads in the 1970's.

FAST AS NASTASE WITHOUT THE RACKET.

MINI

THE NEW QUIET MINIS

Austin Morris
with Supercover

The limited edition Mini Park Lane – far from Sir Alec's idea of the 'peoples car'.

Bringing comfort to the interior was high on the list of priorities. The He-man front seat extensions gave the driver two more inches of leg room for £1 16s 0d. Remote gear changes to replace the 'magic wand' gear change cost between £7 and £25 depending on complexity. Door handles easily replaced the standard string pulls on some cars for 10s and a wood grained plastic dash made a smarter dash for £1 12s 6d. Early improvements also tried to make the most of the Mini's small size. The LMB glass fibre boot extension added a Elf/Hornet type back for £25 5s or if this was not to your liking, perhaps you would have prefered fitted cases for the boot by S Reid Ltd at £9 10s and a Harper fibreglass roof rack for £27 for the other bits and pieces. For the really extravagant, a Webasto sun roof for £66 8s and Linton wind up window conversions for £12 per side were available.

As the Mini cult began to gain momentum, owners wanted to make their cars look different on the outside. Peter Sellers made wickerwork down the side of the car popular and you too could have the 'continental look' for just 18s 11d per yard. Whilst at it, a sticker to flaunt your Mini's agility to other car owners reading 'You have just been Mini'd' was a snip at 5d post paid. This did no good to the standing of the Mini owner. *Autocar* 10 July 1964 referred to Mini Hooligans and concluded 'Driving a Mini certainly causes one to adopt a different and distinctive attitude, but, we believe, no more than would any compact little car that can take advantage of smaller openings and its superior manoeuvrability. Human nature being what it is, the temptation to exceed one's rights in these matters is strong'. In the same magazine legendary tuner Daniel Richmond who ran Downton Engineering said 'It must be said that a lot of feelings are engendered by the incredibly bad manners of a small section of Mini drivers. These abuse the roadholding, acceleration and compact dimensions to perform antics which often appear much more dangerous than they really are, but which nevertheless arouse hostile feelings in the drivers of larger cars. The same people are also inclined to find an outlet for their exhibitionism by making their cars look as though they think a racing Mini should appear, with plastic numbers, chequered tape, number discs, noisy exhausts and the like, and the net result gives both the car and the conversion industry a bad name'. Later in the 1960's looking sporty was even more popular with 4.5 inch Cosmic alloy wheels at five for £40 19s, a Scorpion stream-lined front end to fit over the existing wings for £40 19s, metal trims to fit over the existing plastic wheel spokes for £1 and Masemco slip on seat covers with bucket seat look padded sides at £6 6s each.

Although the Mini accessory business declined during the 1970's and tastes have changed, there is still a wide range of fairly cheap products the Mini owner can buy to personalise his or her car.

Opposite page
Ritz – another LE Mini.

Above
Advantage – anyone for tennis?

Following pages
Redhot and Jetblack.

Mary Quant in her 'Designer' Mini.

The Mini Piccadilly in its native environ-
ment.

Below
Mini 25, celebrating 25 years of the Mini in 1984 with Miss Mini 25.

Right
Mini 25 interior was the most luxurious production Mini until launch of Mini Thirty.

Above
The basic Mini City gives excellent value for money.

Opposite above
Mini Mayfair gives luxury at reasonable cost.

Right
From the start accessories were numerous for the Mini.

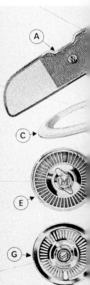

A   STYLA Radiator Grille, Anodised Aluminium, complete with Medallion A or M. SRG.I.

B   STYLA Spotlight, moveable. Chrome Plated Brass. SSP.IA.

C   STYLA Tyre Trims. Pure White Rubber. Set of four. STT.7.

D   STYLA Spinners, SP.6. Anodised Aluminium, complete with Medallions A or M. Set of four.

E   STYLA Flyte Discs. Anodised Aluminium, complete with Red Background. SP.6 Spinners and Medallions A or M. Set of four. SFD.7.

F   STYLA Spinners, SP.I. Chrome Plated Brass, complete with STYLA Medallions. Set of four.

G   STYLA Sportsdiscs. Anodised Aluminium, complete with STYLA Medallions. Set of four. SAD.7.

H   STYLA Turbine Discs. Anodised Aluminium, complete with SP.6 Spinners and Medallions A or M. Set of four. STD.7.

I   STYLA Clearvue. Anti-condensation Shield 10" x 25" Each. SAC.I.

J   STYLA Spotlamp. Chrome Plated Brass, complete with Bracket. Each. SSP.2.

K   STYLA Spinners, SP.3. Chrome Plated Brass, complete with STYLA Medallions. Set of four.

L   STYLA Spinners, SP.4. Chrome Plated Brass, complete with STYLA Medallions. Set of four.

M   STYLA Spinners, SP.2. Chrome Plated Brass, complete with STYLA Medallions. Set of four.

N   STYLA Stainless Steel Strip. Complete with Clips. Set of six, SSS.MA.1.

O   STYLA Tailor-made Mudflaps. Pure White Rubber, complete with fixing brackets. Pair. SMFT.6W.

P   STYLA Universal Mudflaps. Pure Rubber, complete with Anodised Aluminium Decor and necessary fixing brackets. Pair. SMF.3W. Gold or Chrome.

Q   STYLA Chrome Strip, 2 in. Mylar Plastic Chrome Strip, self-adhesive. 25 ft. rolls.

R   STYLA Chrome Strip, 1 in. Mylar Plastic Chrome Strip, self-adhesive. 25 ft. rolls.

S   STYLA Chevrons, 2 in. Chrome or Gold. Set of six. SC.1C or SC.1G.

T   STYLA "M.1" Anti-vibration Mirror. Chrome Plated Brass. Each. SM.2.

U   STYLA Universal Mudflaps. Standard Black Rubber. Pair. SMF.1B.

*V STYLA Tailor-made Mudflaps. Black Rubber with White Inserts. Pair. SMFT.6B.

W   STYLA Tailor-made Mudflaps. Black Rubber, complete with Reflector. Pair. SMFT.6R.

* Also with word 'Mini' embossed on flap

Above
1960 Austin fitted with vintage extras.

Below
Spare wheel on outside leaves more room in the boot.

Right
The extras also cover the interior.

The men

The Mini's creator Alexander Arnold Constantine Issigonis was born on November 18th 1906, the same year in which Herbert Austin launched his first car from Longbridge, a 20 horsepower chain driven vehicle which was techonologically a long way from a modern motorcar. In his working lifetime Issigonis changed many concepts in vehicle design and his ideas are now part of modern car design. Issigonis has been described as a 'man for his time'; indeed it is fair to say that the motor industry will probably never produce a designer like him again. What must be rembered is that although Issigonis had a design team, at the end of the day he made the decisions and bore the responsibility.

The Mini was Issigonis's child even though many people have played a part in its maturity. Issigonis was 53 when the Mini was launched and already an important man within BMC being answerable only to the Managing Director. So what then had led him to the position where he could create the Mini in his own way? The answer is perhaps threefold; practicality, born out of a tough background; experience, gained in his years in the motor business and perhaps just as important, arrogance in his own ability.

Although Issigonis was born into a fairly wealthy family, which owned a marine engineering company, his formative years were not easy ones. Issigonis was born in Smyrna, now called Izmir, part of Turkey and around 200 miles from Istanbul. The young Alex had his mind fixed on being an engineer from an early age. However, the family business was taken over by the Germans during World War I when

One of the more unusual extras.

Left
For a long time wheel arches have been very popular.

Right
Even new cars also get the special treatment.

Alex's father refused to help repairing U boats. After the war was over, Greece was given the land along the coast in which Smyrna stood and the family business was restored to them but in 1922 Turkish troops invaded. British nationals including the Issigonises were evacuated to Malta by the Royal Navy. Penniless again, Alec's tough childhood continued as his father died whilst living as a refugee in Malta. At the age of 16 Alec and his mother set off for England. Needless to say his turbulent childhood meant he had very little formal education so he enrolled at the Battersea Polytechnic to do a three year engineering course. Issigonnis's biggest struggle was his mathematics, mainly because he hated it so much, believing mathematics was uncreative. However, he eventually passed his exams and left the college. With this difficult upbringing, it is not surprising that in his later life Issigonis was interested in making the most of what you had and bringing motoring to the masses rather than to the lucky few.

His experience was gained both in the motor industry and in his private life. When he left college his mother bought him as his first car a Singer Saloon. Alec and his mother set off on a tour of Europe in the Singer. No doubt this experience must

have had some influence on his later design ideas.

He also learnt from his own racing experience driving the Issigonis lightweight Special. Aged 22, his first job was as a draughtsman in a small London engineering firm. In 1934 he joined the design team of Humber and two years later he was head-hunted by Morris, at that time the biggest car manufacturing Company in Britain. He started at Cowley in Oxfordshire designing rear axles. Alec wanted wider responsibilities and over the next few years his persistance paid off as he was allowed more time to work on his own ideas. Eventually he had his own team working on a completely new vehicle. Issigonis laboured at his ideas for the Morris Minor throughout the war. The Minor was launched in 1948 and became the first British car with sales of over a million.

In 1952 Morris Motors merged with the Austin Motor Company to form the British Motor Corporation (BMC). Issigonis was unhappy with the new set-up and moved to Alvis where he designed a sports saloon. However, Alvis did not accept the design and four years work was scrapped. Issigonis designed the car from scratch and no doubt this added a great deal to his design experience. Issigonis returned to BMC by invitation of the Chairman Leonard Lord and was again head of his own design team. Later that year the Suez Crisis broke when Egypt cut the oil pipeline supplying the West. This lead to petrol rationing in Europe. Foreign car makers were quick to capitalise on this and small economical 'bubble' cars were seen on the British street.

Issigonis' belief in himself had been demonstrated earlier. Whilst he was working on the Minor, everyone else was working on big luxury cars in anticipation of a post-war boom. He was in a rush with the Mini and expected maximum output from his team and woe-betide anyone who got the wrong side of him. All those who worked with him had to get used to his way of working which was very graphic, showing complex ideas in the form of scribbled notes on any piece of paper which happened to be at hand. John Cooper can recall having lunch with Issigonis when he started to sketch on the table cloth, eventually leaving with his ideas and the table cloth under his arm. Even when the Mini was in production Issigonis would make sure the workforce were putting the car together properly by walking into a field of Minis, pointing to one at random and saying he wanted to take that one out. Staff at the factory would then put plates on the car, fill it with petrol and bump start it. If he had any problems with the car, somebody was in for a ticking off when he returned.

Issigonis' practicality, experience and self confidence worked. Just sixteen months after the project was started, the car was ready to be presented to Leonard Lord. Issigonis drove Lord around the Longbridge works in the new car and stopped outside Lord's office. History was in the making when Lord turned to Alec and said 'Alec, I want it made in a year's time. Get going!'.

Issigonis went on to design the 1100, 1300, 1800 and Maxi and was by this time one of BMC's greatest assets. He also worked on many less successful ideas such as a steam powered Mini. Steam was a great interest of Issigonis and when he retired he spend much of his time working on model steam trains.

Although his self-confidence had helped with the Mini it did not make him ideally suited to the changing world of car design which was increasingly based on specialist teams working on each part of the car. In 1968 BMC merged with Leyland to form British Leyland. The new boss Lord Stokes had plans and Issigonis was not part of them. For some time before this Issigonis had been working on a Mini replacement, the 9X. It was a more refined Mini-size car with a new feature — a 'hatch back'. However, the 9X project was stopped by Lord Stokes who considered it more important to find a successor for the Maxi as the public were looking for bigger cars. The move to smaller, less fuel consuming cars, was not predicted.

In 1969 Issigonis was knighted for his services to the motor industry and two years later, aged 65, he

Issigonis would be proud that Minis have brought so much fun to people.

This Mayfair shows you can still buy plenty of bits for your Mini.

retired. Most people might receive a gold watch for a retirement gift but not Sir Alec – he wanted and got the biggest Meccano set you could buy. Issigonis was quite bitter about the 9X not going into production, especially when he saw foreign 'hatch backs' dominating the small car market. In 1978, ten years after the project was axed, Issigonis claimed that had the project not been dropped the British car industry would not have been in the trouble it was in.

John Newton Cooper was born in Kingston, Surrey on July 17th 1932, the son of Charles Newton Cooper, a highly respected motor engineer. Aged only twelve he drove a car built for him by his father around Brooklands and capable of doing over 90 mph. On that day he chatted about his modified Austin Seven with a friend by the name of Donald Campbell.

Cooper first met Alec Issigonis in 1946 when Issigonis was racing his 'lightweight Special'. The car was well in advance of its time being a single seater and boasting rubber suspension. Cooper met him a few times in future years but only became friends when Cooper was using A-series engines in formula racing cars. Issigonis would show him designs and later prototypes of the Mini and discuss its development. Cooper drove one of the Mini prototypes to the Italian Grand Prix in 1959 and caused quite a stir. Italian designer Lampredi who was Ferrari's chief designer and later became Fiats chief engineer saw the car and asked to try it. When he returned he said to Cooper 'If that car was not so ugly I would shoot myself' but he added 'That is the future motor car'. As to being ugly he was used to Ferraris

Issigonis working on a steam Mini.

Left
The 'S' that makes all the difference.

Right
John Cooper – still mad about Minis.

Below
The ideal Police pursuit car.

and the Mini's radical looks did need some getting used to.

When Cooper approached Issigonis about tuning the Mini he was not over-keen at first as he believed the Mini was just a practical small car. Cooper pointed out that all the racing drivers and their mechanics had the Mini so why not make 'one for the boys'. Issigonis said 'let's go and ask the headmaster', their nickname for top man at BMC, George Harriman, Harriman's response was to say go on and do it then.

Within two weeks Cooper presented a Mini to Harriman which had a formula Junior A-series engine and discs brakes from Lockheed. After a test drive Harriman said that they should build some but

thought Cooper's idea of doing 1000 was ridiculous as they would never sell that many. When the Mini Cooper was finally dropped, around 150,000 had been made.

Cooper was made a consultant and went to the BMC once a week, race meetings allowing. The first Cooper was relatively simple as Cooper had experience of tuning the A-series but the Cooper S's were

Below
The Mk II Cooper.

Right
By the time of the introduction of Mk II the S had its own badge.

far more complicated with the idea of racing firmly in mind. The experience on the track and in rallies was passed directly onto the factory to aid development. Mini Coopers had great success in motor sport but John Cooper is particularly proud of the three (official) Monte Carlo rally wins as Cooper racing cars also won the Monaco Grand Prix three times.

John Cooper was nearly killed in an accident in a twin-engined Mini. He had been keen to create a twin-engined car for rallying and discussed it with Issigonis who told him he was building a similar vehicle for military use. So the twin-engined Moke and Mini appeared around the same time. The TwiniMoke was a brilliant design beating many other military vehicles in trials but it failed on carrying capacity. BMC got to the stage of being able to enter a twin engined Mini into a rally but when Cooper was nearly killed in his one, Harriman dropped the project immediately. He was not keen from the start as he wanted to race what they sold. To this day Cooper still believes that a twin-engined car was, and still is, viable.

The Cooper Mini was the first performance production saloon and was the link between the old two seater sportscars and the modern so called 'hot hatchback' saloon cars. The Mini Cooper era lasted 10 years during which time John Cooper made £2 per car. When this deal was made, a shake of hands was all that was needed. When the Cooper name was dropped, he was given the excuse that the Cooper name was making the car too expensive to insure but then they called the replacement a GT and the insurance companies thought it was just a Cooper in disguise. The Cooper name continued on the Italian made Innocenti Cooper another three years. It was Lord Stokes who saw the end of the Cooper. His view was that the company had 150,000 employees so why did they need consultants like Cooper? John Cooper even suggested they continue to make Coopers without paying him anything but Stokes was adamant.

The Mk II 'S'

Below
Mk III 'S' – last of the Coopers.

Right
The Innocenti Cooper – in typical European style.

Below Right
Mk III Elf – one of the most luxurious Minis ever built on the production line.

Left
Wood and leather luxury.

Below
Heinz cars at a reunion meeting.

*Radford Mini was a luxury model that
was built to carriage maker's standards.*

Radford styling showing the Mini as a hatchback.

Left
The first Clubman converted by Wood and Pickett.

Above
Wood and Pickett Clubman interior shows the craftsmanship that made these 'WP' Minis famous.

Following pages
The Margrave; a favourite of the rich and famous.

Left
The distinctive WP badge.

Above
Taking the exterior seams off the Mini makes for smoother lines.

Below
WP interior was for many the ultimate luxury.

Right
WP still going strong.

The cars

The Mini has been developed in many ways to add some luxury to the basic interior. Rover Group has launched more and more luxurious Mini variants, rich owners have had specialist firms do the work for them and the everyday owners have put hours in themselves to achieve similar results.

How much the coachbuilt cars have added to the Mini character is arguable. The car was intended to be a car for the people and the number of these high luxury cars in proportion to the total production is minute. However, as has been said, the Mini has become classless and these cars have had some contribution to make. For although some impressed with leather seats and a walnut dashboard the car remains a Mini.

In the 1960's there were a multitude of specialist conversion companies. One notable coach maker was Hooper Motor Services who built Peter Sellers' Cooper with the distinctive wickerwork sides for the mere sum of £2600 (five times the price of a standard Cooper). Crayford Engineering who offered a convertible conversion for £129. Crayford once constructed 57 convertible Hornets for prizes in a Heinz 57 competition. They also built the Viking Hornet Sport convertible which cost £757 and for which you got a mildly tuned engine and 22 luxury refinements.

Perhaps the most famous of these specialists were Harold Radford Ltd and Wood and Pickett. Radford built cars for sheikhs, filmstars and pop idols who did not mind paying over double the standard car price for luxury. Radford built its own standard con-

This de luxe adaptation is home made but BL did consider adding a long boot to the Clubman.

Owners put in hours of work to make their own opulent interiors.

version called the Mini de Ville but would also do just about anything you asked the company to do to your Mini, such as a built-in wash basin with running water, a lady's vanity case with strip-lighting round the dash and even a built-in tape recorder so you could dictate letters as your chauffeur dashed you to the City.

Wood and Pickett was formed by ex-Hooper employees who left after a dispute and unlike many of the specialists conversion companies the company still trades today. By 1969 W&P had built 200 conversions ranging from £1000 to £3500. Amongst its

customers were the Rolling Stones, the Bee Gees and the Aga Khan. The work was top quality and expensive, £110 for a respray, £175 for a dashboard and £185 for electric windows. Like Radford, Wood and Pickett offered a standard conversion called the Margrave but over 70 items were listed on their price list for you to make up your own car. Today a Wood and Pickett Mini with all the refinements is likely to be over four times the cost of a new Mayfair.

As well as making cars look different by adding extras many have been made to look different by altering their shape. Minis have been lowered, made taller, shorter, longer and wider. As well as keen owners with a knack for welding Minis have been

Jaguar seats and dash in a Mini.

altered by specialist conversion companies. The Wildgoose Mini Motorhome was built in Worthing in the 1960's and around 50 were made. Although the idea worked well the price was too high due to the huge amount of work which went into the production of each Wildgoose. Another body alteration carried out by a specialist company, although very different from the Wildgoose, was the Mini Sprint. The Mini Sprint and Mini Sprint GT were built by Stewart and Ardern who were the largest Morris distributors in the world in the late 1960's. What made the cars unusual apart from the deseaming and square headlights was the fact that the bodies of the cars were lowered. The GT had 1.5 inches removed from between floor and waistline, a further 1.5

inches between the waistline and the roof and another 1.25 inches from the roof. Around 150 man-hours went into each car so again the price was prohibitive to the average Mini owner as it was almost twice the price of the base car. Perhaps the best car which falls into this bracket is the Ogle. The Ogle was a sports car body which replaced the original Mini bodywork. Unfortunately only 66 cars were made as the designer David Ogle was killed in one of the cars on the way to Brands Hatch race circuit. Again the car was expensive, the bodywork costing as much as the base Cooper.

Two of the best Mini kits still in production today are the Scamp and the GTM. The Scamp built in Brookwood Surrey is a Moke-type vehicle but with a far finer finish, having many modern car refinements plus plenty of room, particulrly the six wheel model. The GTM made in Loughborough, Leicestershire, tries to develop the Mini into a sportscar. Unlike similar kits, the GTM looks good as well as giving Mini performance and roadholding. Another Mini kit which has a fairly recent history is the Mini Pimlico. The Pimlico is a Mini convertible bodyshell brought up to date.

Another unusual Mini came not from a small specialist firm but a large Italian factory. Innocenti of

The Ogle – one of the best of the special conversions.

Milan, who previously built scooters, were given permission to produce the standard Mini under licence in 1965. The cars sold well, so much so that British Leyland took control of Innocenti is 1972. BL introduced the Bertone styled hatch back in 1974, the 998 cc being called the 90 and the 1275 cc the 120. However, BL pulled out of the operation due to mounting losses. The company was taken over by the late Alexandro De Tomaso who added large bumpers, alloy wheels and an air scoop on the bonnet to give it a more sporty feel.

The cult of the Mini has spread around the world but in many countries, the Mini's popularity amongst its owners is even keener than in the UK because the car is so much rarer. What is unusual is that different aspects of the car and its character have come

to the fore in different countries. In Europe, in particular Germany where there are some 30 Mini Clubs, the Minis are often highly customised. European Minis tend to be sheep in wolves clothing because legislation stops almost all engine modifications. Time and money is spent in making the car look beautiful. Big wheels, body kits, fancy spray work and big stereos typify these Minis. As far as the sale of new Minis is concerned France is the biggest market outside the UK.

In the USA there are said to be around 5,000 Minis. There are a number of clubs but the Mini never caught on in the States despite many attempts to establish them. America never accepted the Mini although it did accept the VW Beetle.

Minis were fairly popular in Australia and were indeed made there. The Morris 850 was produced in Australia and assembled from British parts from 1961 to 1964. The Cooper was introduced in 1963 and the S in 1965. Unlike Britain when the GT was introduced, it used the S engine, twin carburettors and all. Production of Minis in Australia finished with the Clubman 1275LS. 400 of these cars were produced in gold and silver to mark the end of the Aussie Mini. Minis were also fairly popular in New Zealand. The 1980 New Zealand Film Corporation film 'Good Bye Pork Pie' featured a yellow Mini which raced from one side of the country to the other followed by the police. This film is recommended viewing for all Mini enthusiasts.

Perhaps the keenest Mini buyers overseas today are the Japanese who buy all Austin Rover can ship

The Wildgoose Motorhome was too expensive to sell in large numbers.

Below
It's name says it all, 'Short but Sweet'.

Right
A Mini not for the shy.

Left
Another one-off Mini creation.

Right
This Mini lives up to its name of 'Austin tatious'.

Below
Welded into the back of this Mini are 8 inches of extra metal which produce this unusual effect.

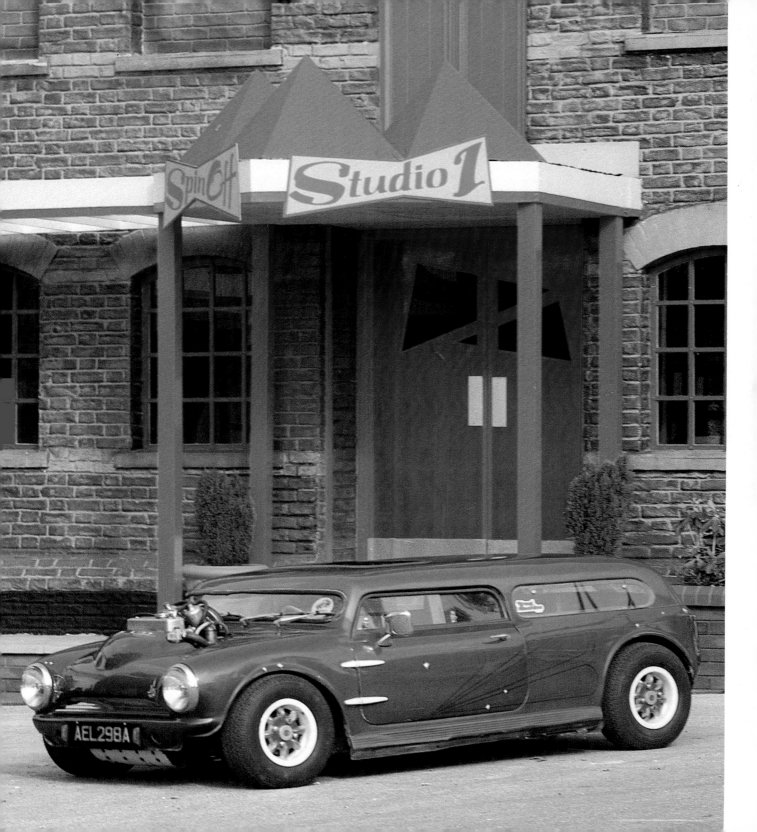

Left
Claustrophobia – claimed to be the world's lowest car that is road-going.

Above
This half-scale replica named 'Mini Mouse' was built for a school project.

to them. They are also interested in older models and Coopers in particular. Unlike the Europeans the Japanese like their cars as basic and original looking as possible. They even take out modern Mayfair fittings and replace them with more period fitments

such as the oval clock cluster in the middle of the dash.

The development of the Mini as a sporting car has played an immense part in the creation of the Mini character.

Motoring enthusiasts were quick to discover the versatility of the Mini for all forms of competition and the ease with which they could be modified. It was these enthusiasts who started the Mini Se7en Club in the early 1960's. By 1965 ordinary saloon racing was becoming expensive for the club's members, so the Mini Se7en Formula was born – the ultimate in lost cost racing. From its modest start it grew well and by the end of the 1966 season there were about

70 drivers. In 1969 a halfway stage between the Mini 7 and the full blown saloon cars was introduced by the formation of the 1-litre Mini Miglia Formula.

In 1976 Leyland Cars (now Rover Group) offered backing for both formulae in exchange for the club administering Leyland's 1275GT Challenge races. The previously weak Mini Miglia class now renamed Mini 1000 developed into a closely fought, and increasingly more professional national status championship. While the Mini 7's, despite remaining basically a 'fun' formula, benefitted from their smarter image to attract more attention then ever before. The 1275's

The GTM is an outstanding Mini kit car.

came and went but the Mini 7 and the renamed Mini Miglia Formula went into the 1980's as the strongest purely amatuer classes in British racing. By the mid-eighties better tyres, suspensions and engine building, called for action to endeavour to slow down the cars. Although limitations were made on the engines all the cars are getting quicker and lap times are still being broken. Despite the reasonably tight regulations, a good Mini 7 can expect about 85–90 bhp at the flywheel, with a top speed in the region of 120 mph.

The Mini's good roadholding is put to the test is Minicross racing. The sport was started around ten years ago when a small advertisement called for competitors to take part in a new grasstrack formula.

Minicross cars are based on 850cc cars with limited modifications allowed. Racing is normally on an oval track marked out on a field. Drivers are graded according to past performances, with the fastest driver at the back of the starting grid. With this and fairly standard cars, racing is close and exciting.

The Mini as a rally car (like the racing cars) added a great deal to the Mini character, with the cheeky little Mini beating the bigger cars. The height of this was the series of Monte Carlo wins mentioned earlier. In 1964 Paddy Hopkirk won in a 1071 Cooper S and 1965 saw Timo Makinen win in a 1275 S. Makinen's Mini was amongst only 35 cars that finished the rally out of 237 starters as there were terrible weather conditions. Minis were in first, second

and third place in 1966 but an exceptional bit of French partisanship put a Citroën in front after disqualifying the Minis and a Lotus Cortina which finished fourth on a technicality about lights after more than a day's scrutinising. Simply, the French just could not believe the humble Mini could beat Porsche and Saab. The disqualifications hit the front page of the papers in England and created untold publicity for the cars. John Cooper most concerned at the news from France phoned George Harriman at BMC, who just replied "What's wrong we won didn't we?" There was talk of boycotting the 1967

Rear of a GTM shows the engine compartment.

Monte Carlo but BMC wanted another chance to show the Mini could be world beater. It took a masterly display of driving by Rauno Aaltonen to finish just 13 seconds in front of a Lancia. Of course, the Monte wins are the most famous but the works teams had many other successes.

In modern terms the works S's were not very dissimilar to what you could buy from the dealer but you could for an extra £550 buy a car with the full BMC works team specification. If this was too much you could choose from a list of parts from an auxiliary lamp bar for £6 to an engine for £250. The works cars now are very sought after, one car being sold for over £10,000 but many owners have to do with replicas in the distinctive works red and white paint schemes.

Below.
The Hustler kit car in six-wheel form.

Right
Innocenti range showing both ordinary Mini shape and the Bertone styled hatchback.

Below right
The Innocenti 120 converted into a Cabriolet.

Left
Interior of the Innocenti 120.

Above
The racy Innocenti de Tomaso.

Below left
The Mini from the New Zealand film
'Good Bye Pork Pie'.

Below
An uncommon encounter.

エクステリアで主張するあなただけのミニに、街が注目。

ミニは小さい。だからそのままでも充分に可愛いい。しかし、ミニは小さい。だからどんなにドレスアップしても、決して下品でなく可愛いい、とも言えるのではないか。

そしてもう一つ、ミニのドレスアップの特長としてあげられることは、そのパーツの多くが長い栄光の歴史に根差して作られていることだ。あなたは一体いつのモンテカルロを、どこのサーキットをイメージしてミニを飾るのか——100人には100種類のミニがある。

●アルミホイール5J×12インチ1本 ¥25,000
ミニクーパーがレースやラリーで現役だった頃、ミニライトと呼ばれる素っ気ない程シンプルなデザインのホイールが良く使われた。これはそれの12インチ版として作られたレプリカ。正統的アイテムの筆頭だ。

●GTフェンダーミラー（左右あり）1コ ¥4,000
ドアミラーが全盛の今だからこそ、フェンダーミラーが光る。むかしのボーイズレーサーは、みんなコイツにあこがれていたものだ。

●メッキドアミラー
1コ ¥3,200（左右あり）
クルマが小さい分だけ、ドアミラーは派手にする——それもオシャレだ。曲面鏡を採用した広い視野も魅力。粘着テープ止めの他、ハードな走りに安心なビス止め式もある。

●サンハッチ ¥60,000（シーラント¥6,000）
陽射しをあびて走るのは、いつでも気持ちがいい。後端をチルトさせれば、ベンチレーション効果も申し分なし。

●マークⅡメッキグリル ¥26,000
●ワンタッチグリルボタン ¥2,500
モンテカルロで活躍した頃のグリルと、当時整備性を考えて使われたグリル脱着用ボタン。クーパーSの顔になる。

●アンダーガード‥‥‥M/T車用 ¥19,500
A/T車用 ¥22,000
車高の低いミニでダートを攻めるなら、絶対にこれだけは取り付けたい実質的なアクセサリー。もちろんモンテカルロで勝ったワークスカーも、同様のものを採用していた。

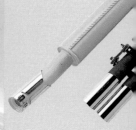

●ルーキプラバムマフラー（S）
●アバルトマフラー（W）‥‥‥‥¥
●アンサマフラー（W）‥‥‥‥‥¥

MAKE YOUR OW

●オーバーフェンダー5丁ブラック‥¥17,000
クーパーS風にキメるなら、ぜひとも欲しいド
レスアップ・パーツ。走りのイメージが、いち
だんとヒカる。

●BOSCHフォグランプ 1ヶ¥9,000
霧の向うにボッシュが光り、やがて
ミニが見えて来る。対向車唖然。

●オーバーライダー1コ‥‥‥‥‥¥12,000
●オーバーライダーパイプ4本セット¥24,000
これも、クーパーS仕様には欠かせない魅力
的なパーツ。外観がいちだんと引き締まり、
ハンサム・ミニに。

●リヤワイパーキット‥‥‥‥‥‥¥15,000
かつてのミニオーナーは、ほとんどといって
よいほど装着していた。視認性の向上と、
リヤのアクセントに最適です。

〈アクセサリーパーツの価格に、取り付け工賃は含まれておりません。〉

質で選ぶか、ルックスで選ぶかは自由だ。い
れを選んでも、チューニングの第一歩とし
の価値は充分にある一流品だ。

N Mini

The future

No matter what the future brings nothing can take away the Mini's achievements. The car which set the way towards modern car design, sold millions, lasted years and along the way collected the title of perhaps the best known car in the world.

Rover Group have made it clear that whilst the Mini is still popular and there is a market for it they will continue to sell it. However, the development of motoring law and the restrictions on car design are catching up with the Mini. It will be a bureaucrat who decides that the Mini has had its lot.

Left
Austin Rover Japan supply parts to make Minis look older than they are.

Below
Interior of a Mini Miglia racing car.

In conclusion, the Mini regardless of when it ceases production will last forever if the enthusiasm owners have put into helping with this book is a guide.

John Cooper remembers a lunch he had with Issigonis and the stylist Farina who worked for BMC. Issigonis was arguing with Farina about design and blasted at Farina "Your Car with its fins will last till next year and then it will be out of style – MY CAR WILL LAST FOREVER!"

Above
FUMIN into the bend.

Right
Take off!

Above right
Minicross in action.

Left
*The plastic windscreen with holes in
helps when the mud starts flying.*

Below
*This dragster Mini is capable of doing a
quarter mile in 11.49 seconds and is
powered by a 4.7 litre Chevrolet engine.*

Following pages
*A works team Cooper in action on the
1967 Monte Carlo Rally.*

Preceding pages
Another of the works team cars.

Below
The cockpit of a works car.

Right
A restored works car which has been driven by such famous rally drivers as Hopkirk and Aaltonen.

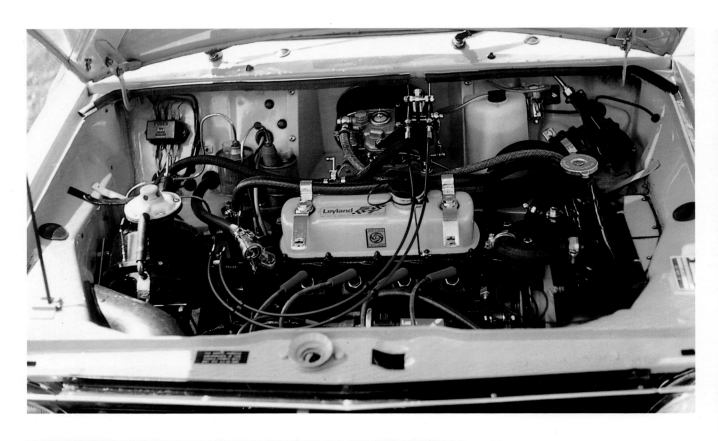

Above
Owners of ordinary road going cars are also keen to increase the power of their Minis. This engine bay has been subtly modified.

Right
Even Mokes are built for performance.

Left
Cross-flow head with carbs and exhaust opposite side on the fast Moke.

Deceivingly standard looks.

Left
A 1600 cc Lotus engine shoehorned into the engine bay gives top speed of over 130 mph.

Above
Modern re-styling for the Mini using a Kat styling kit.

Wide and low and with a surprise.

Above
Owning a Mini sometimes calls for a sense of humour.

Right
What Mini driving is all about.